My Sheep Will Know My Voice

(Hearing and Discerning God's Voice)

by Robin Moore Joyce

REJOYCE MOORE MINISTRIES

Scripture quotations marked (Amp) are taken from *The Amplified Bible*, Copyright © 1987 by The Zondervan Corporation and the Lockman Foundation. All rights reserved.

Scripture quotations marked (NIV) are taken from *The Quest Study Bible*, New International Version ® Copyright © 1994 by The Zondervan Corporation. All rights reserved.

Scripture quotations marked (KJ) are taken from the King James Version of the Bible.

Cited excerpts are from *Hearing from God* (previously titled *Listening Prayer*) by Mary Ruth Swope, copyright 1987, and used by permission of the publisher, Whitaker House, New Kensington, PA.

MY SHEEP WILL KNOW MY VOICE
ISBN 0-9722577-0-5
Copyright © 2002 by Robin Moore Joyce
Rejoyce Moore Ministries, Inc.
428 Cokain Road
Harrisville, PA 16038
814-786-9358

All rights reserved under International Copyright Law. Contents and/or cover may not be reproduced in whole or in part in any form without express written consent of the publisher.

Printed in the U.S.A. by Beacon Litho
401 Erie Street
Grove City, PA 16127
724-458-5086

Dedication

Bob Joyce and Blanky Moore

Thank you for being a light in a lost and dying world. It was the love of God shining so brightly in both of you that illuminated the pathway to Jesus. I praise God for you.

Acknowledgment

Mary Ruth Swope

Thank you for writing a book that taught me how to hear and discern the voice of God.

Table of Contents

	Preface	iii
1	The Convenience Store	1
	Voice of God	4
	Father God	5
2	You Mean There's More?	7
	Praying in the Spirit	10
3	The Garden of Eden	13
	Love Walk	16
	The Heart, the Vine, and the Gardener	17
	The Heart	19
4	I Say They Are There	23
5	God's Faithful Servant	27
	He Is the Potter	30
	My Now Identity	32
6	A Living Testament	35
	Prayer	38
7	God Has A Plan	41
8	Find My Socks!	45
9	Salvation	49
	Glory, Grace, and Mercy	53
	Eternal Salvation	55
	Eternity–Everlasting Life	56
10	New Life	59
	Transformation through His Spirit	61
	The Seed	62

11	Slow Down!	65
	God's Beast of Burden	*67*
12	To Know About Each Other	71
	Hidden Pride	*74*
	Love and Correction	*75*
13	To Know Each Other	79
14	Listening Prayer	83
15	The Wrong Spirit	85
	Engrafted Word of God	*88*
16	Discerning God's Voice	91
	This Property Under Construction	*95*
	Special Commentary	*97*
17	The Desires of Thine Heart	101
18	Practicing Listening Prayer	105
19	You Can Hear	109
	The Light of the World	*112*

Preface

This book is a gift from God and sent for many to understand that God is waiting to speak to them through His Spirit. Not long after my salvation, I became aware that God was working to help me understand without a doubt that He wanted to speak with me. He put a passion in me to examine His Word for evidence that He desired to speak clearly and specifically about His plans and His purposes.

As I came to hear God's voice more clearly, I began to receive messages that I lovingly call "God Mail." At first, I wrote them by hand but later typed them on the computer. They were often about events or concepts that I was struggling with concerning my new life with God. I found them enlightening, inspiring, and encouraging. Eventually, I received messages for others and saw them truly blessed. God was using these messages to help me and others understand His ways. Some of these messages have been included at the ends of various chapters to help clarify how it was I became so sure of who I am in Jesus Christ and how much God loves me. I hope that they will do the same for you. I believe they will. *(Note: Scriptural references were added later by Bob and me to confirm the messages.)*

Chapter One

The Convenience Store

"My sheep will know My voice" were words that resonated in my brain one morning as I was seeking God in prayer. God led me to the Scripture concerning this. In John 10, I found much of the evidence I needed to secure my belief that God wanted to speak to me clearly. The voice I heard sounded much like mine, but the thoughts had wisdom and strength only God could possess. John 10:3-4 (NIV) says,

> *The watchman opens the gate for him, and the sheep listen to his voice. He calls his own sheep by name and leads them out. When he has brought out all his own, he goes on ahead of them, and his sheep follow him because they know his voice.*

After reading John 10 several times, the words began to leap off the pages and into my heart. I could sense that God was giving me the knowledge and the assurance I needed to believe that He would speak to me.

God's voice was not really a voice at the start. It was receiving knowledge through thoughts that were unlike my own. I had read from so many in ministries and from the only true source, the Bible, that God would speak to me. The Bible says in Romans 8:5, 6, and 14 (NIV),

> *Those who live according to the sinful nature have their minds set on what that nature desires; but those who live in accordance with the Spirit have their minds set on what the Spirit desires. The mind of sinful man is death, but the mind controlled by the Spirit is life and peace ... because those who are led by the Spirit of God are sons of God.*

However, I constantly questioned whether I was truly hearing from God, or was I just engaging in whimsical thinking? *I mean, me, hearing from the Creator of the universe.* But as time passed, I became sure that He really was speaking to me.

As His still quiet voice became more of a presence in prayer and throughout my day, I became convinced that this was the voice of God. In one instance I was standing in a convenience store checkout line, and God gave me a knowing that I should allow a man behind me to go ahead of me. Well, there was only one person in front of us, and I had only one item. So I rationalized to myself that it was not necessary to let him go ahead of me. As it turned out, the events that followed showed me, without question, that God spoke to protect me and to bless another.

Just as I had reasoned, the line went quickly and smoothly, and I was out of the store not more than a minute later. I got in my car, started backing out of the parking area, and bumped into a car that had been hidden from my view. That car was waiting for a place at the gas pump. When I hit the car, my heart sank, and I immediately got out to examine the damage. While I was apologizing to the person whose car I hit, the man who had been in line behind me walked out of the store. I watched as this man, whom God had asked me to bless, walked to his car that was parked in front of the gas pump. The person whose car I had hit had been waiting for that space.

In a split second, the revelation of the series of events became crystal clear. God showed me that if I had been obedient to His voice, He could have used me by blessing one person, and He could have prevented me from denting another person's car.

Thank God for His wonderful patience and love. He turned all things for good. This lesson on obedience (hearing and accepting His guidance) began a hunger and a thirst in me to discover how to hear from our God Almighty. Amen and to Him be all the praise and the honor.

God Mail: Voice of God (John 10)

I am here. The Lord God Almighty is here, and Jesus, the Son and Lord of your heart and soul, is with you also. Come to Me, and I will give you refuge. Come to Me, and I will give you what you need. It is through Me that your desires are met. You can trust that I love you and keep you all the days of your life—without fail. Be of great joy and peace.

It is here each morning that you and I become close, and it is here that you learn more about Me. You expect to hear from Me each morning, and so it is. It is your expectations that cause this to be. You expect your Father in heaven to speak, and so it is. It is not your will but your expectancy that has caused this to be. Your expectancy is great, and it is not in doubt. That is what causes results—that one expects from God based on the truth of God's Word. You know that the Word says, "My sheep will know My voice," so you expect this based on that Word. God speaks to His children and wants to on a consistent basis. But so few know or understand this. They see a distant God—unapproachable and unavailable. They must learn that I wait to speak, but so few take the time to understand that their Father in heaven wants to speak. Help people to be open to the fact that I wish to speak to them. They can come to Me, and I will answer. Be the one to tell of My love and tender mercy toward all who believe. This is the way it is to be, but so few have this revelation of their God.

God Mail: Father God
(Message from the Son)

This is a message from the Son, the Lord Jesus Christ, about the Father. This is acceptable to receive a message from the Son. The Son of God and God the Father are one and the same. (See John 10: 30) No concern to separate is necessary. You will know both as the same. I speak today as one who loves the Father, and I tell you He is great and mighty. He is worthy of praise and of honor.

This is the time for making a commitment to the Father to follow after Him and to not get weary. He is your only spiritual Father in Whom you can trust all things. Be joyful knowing that with Him all things are possible. Love Him always and make Him first in your life, and all things will be done. He is the only One in Whom to place your faith, hope, and trust, for He is the only One Who can promise joy and happiness. He is the only One in Whom can be found total fulfillment and peace. Live in the knowledge that all things are possible with your heavenly Father, and without Him there will be no peace–no rest. Live under His shelter and His protection, and He will make a good way for all those who rest in Him. (See Psalm 91) Be with Him, share with Him, cast your cares on Him, and He will deliver peace of mind. Be sure that all is good in Him, and be sure that only His love is given. He is mighty and great and all-powerful. He will give His anointed power to those who know and love Him and spend time in His presence. He will entrust much to those who adore Him and trust in Him. Love Him with all your heart, and He will lift you up and make you whole. Be with Him, and He will share the wisdom to know Him better. Be His servant and serve. Show Him devotion, love, respect, and admiration. Hold Him in great esteem. He is worthy of all this and more. Love Him and spend time in His presence, for it pleases Him. Praise and worship Him, and He will be with you. Love and honor Him. He loves you and wants to show you great things. Be with Him and walk with Him, and He will be with you. See Him as a Father of love and of kindness. Make Him big and mighty in your heart and your mind, for that is what He is. Walk with Him daily. He should be ever present in your thoughts, deeds, and words. Be a part of Him; do not separate from Him. His will is to have you close by seeking Him. Be faithful and wish to do His will. He will guide and direct you. Be assured that He is with you always and forever. Listen to Him, and do His will. Be available to Him, open to Him, so He can use you as He wills. Do His work with joy and with gratitude. Live as He wills you to live according to His Word, and your joy will be complete. Do His work, and He will reward you with peace, rest, and joy.

These are the things My Father wishes of those who serve Him. He is worthy to be praised and is great beyond comprehension. Grace and mercy are His to give, and He gives freely. It is your choice to take His gift. Do the work of My Father, and you will see your life become more than you imagined.

Chapter Two

You Mean There's More?

Just a few months after accepting the Lord Jesus Christ as my personal Savior, another significant, life-altering event took place in my Christian walk. While attending a Bible conference in Cleveland, Ohio, the Bible teacher spoke about the "baptism with the Holy Spirit." Well, I perked up to listen to this because I was anxious to hear anything that concerned the Holy Spirit.

She told the crowd of thousands that upon salvation the Holy Spirit came to live in our spirit, but He occupied only one room in us. However, if we received the baptism with the Holy Spirit, we would be totally immersed in God's Spirit and endued with power. That was all I needed to hear. I figured that if having the Holy Spirit in just one room was this great, being totally saturated with Him would be beyond what I could imagine.

Therefore, at the end of the conference, my mother and I, along with 350 others, were taken to a smaller auditorium to receive this wonderful gift. We were led in prayer and then instructed to simply receive. Spontaneously, out of the mouths of at least 200 people, came the evidence that we had been baptized with the Holy Spirit. That evidence was our personal prayer language known as "speaking in tongues." I was thrilled, as was my mother. We could have flown home; we were soaring so high. However, the next morning when I tried to speak in my new prayer language, I could not. I felt sick. I cried, thinking I had imagined the whole thing. But thank God for my husband who immediately found Scriptures for me to anchor my belief that I was to have this gift. In Acts 1:5 (NIV) it clearly states, *"For John baptized with water, but in a few days you will be baptized with the Holy Spirit."* Also, in Acts 2:4 (NIV) it says, *"All of them were filled with the Holy Spirit and began to speak in other tongues as the Spirit enabled them."*

As I read over Scriptures such as these, I could feel faith rise up within my spirit. We decided to meet with close pastor friends to pray together about my prayer language. We jumped on our motorcycles, and as we rode along, I had a talk with God. I reminded Him of His Word. I told Him that I believed I had received the baptism and that I expected the next words from my mouth to be my prayer language. And just as I believed, this wonder gift flowed out of my mouth. I was crying and laughing and also speaking in this strange new language as I rode along on my motorcycle. Then I become acutely aware of how this must have appeared. As a car passed me, the passenger in that car turned around to look at me. Ignoring him, I praised God and thanked Him for this exciting new life He gave Me.

What this experience made me realize was that Satan truly does come to steal, kill, and destroy. I could see the Scripture in Matthew manifested. In Matthew 13:19 it warns that as soon as the seed is planted, Satan comes to steal that seed. Also, Matthew 11:12 (Amp) says,

> ... *the kingdom of heaven has endured violent assault, and the violent men seize it by force [as a precious prize—a share in the heavenly kingdom is sought with most ardent zeal and intense exertion].*

I saw clearly that if I were going to progress in the gifts and in the revelations of God, this growth would take time and effort. I must read, meditate, and act upon the Word of God for His Word to have its way. Praise God for His Word!

God Mail: Praying in the Spirit

Yes, Jesus is Lord. I will continue to say this as it gives you great comfort. You have asked Me to teach you to pray.... You seek revelation knowledge of how to pray, and you will be asked to find support in My Word for what I am about to share.

I am going to give you a better understanding of the Holy Spirit with regard to your prayer language.... You received a powerful gift the day you let My Spirit have full reign in your life. You yielded completely to the will of the Father, and His Spirit filled you full to overflowing. So you received a new tongue in which to pray to the Father. It was a language foreign to your ears, but it was powerful in what it made available to you. With this language, you are able to access the very heart of God. The heart of God is the Son, so by speaking out in this tongue, it is the voice of Jesus I hear. You speak as My son would speak. I hear My son in the prayers of the Spirit. (See II Corinthians 3:17-18, John 1:1, 2, and 14)

You have groanings that cannot be uttered in your natural voice, but the Spirit makes intercession in those times. The spirit of you and the Spirit of God are interlocked. You yield in those times completely to let My Spirit have full reign to pray prayers of intercession for the lost and for the downhearted. Those times are powerful. You can trust that it is not your emotions but that it is the prayers of the Spirit of God at work. You can trust this is acceptable. (See John 16:5-15)

You Mean There's More?

I also will speak concerning the work of the Spirit. The Spirit of God is in you to work the Father's will for your life, so there are also prayers for the one to whom the Spirit was given. You are prayed for in those times. You have a strong will, yet you allow the Spirit of God to have His way. That is good. The Spirit of God never forces, but as you yield your own will, My will is done in you and through you.... Just as you have heard, there needs to be balance between the prayers of the righteous and the prayers of their spirit man. The time has come that more learn of this balance. Too much of one or the other is not good. But to strike a balance between the two is necessary. (See I Corinthians 14:14-15)

You have found that prayer can be fun by finding that balance. Too many have found prayer time boring and hard because they have not the balance necessary to do what is required in prayer. Your mind alone cannot keep you in My presence. Your will alone cannot keep you focused on the One to Whom you pray. Your thoughts cannot fathom the purposes and the reasons for prayer. But My Spirit knows the how's and the why's of prayer. My Spirit knows whom to pray for on any given day.... Remember Paul's question: "So what shall I do?" His answer was to pray with his spirit, and also pray with understanding.

Chapter Three

The Garden of Eden

The Lord has blessed me with boldness. Of course, my boldness is based on who I am in Christ Jesus. I am a child of God and a daughter seeking after my Father with *all my heart*. And that is the key to hearing from God. It is all about the condition of one's heart.

One day after I began to hear clearly from God, He showed me the condition of my heart before salvation. He said that when He first saw it, it was a desert wasteland. Nothing of value was able to grow in the soil of my heart. As He was telling me this, I began to see that heart. I saw the wind blowing over it and saw that nothing could withstand that wind. The topsoil had been blown away, and the erosion had formed great crevices. I knew that these deep, wide openings on my heart were scars caused by living a life without God.

But then He showed me the condition of my heart after He came to live in it. He spoke to me about the time He spent plowing the soil of my heart and spreading the needed fertilizer upon it. Once the soil was no longer hard and rocky and was rich with nutrients, it was ready to receive the seed. I saw how He had watered the seed and made the desert into a beautiful, lush green garden. Then, all of a sudden, it struck me that what He was showing me was the Garden of Eden. The garden that was once physically here on the earth was now in the hearts of all those who believe and receive His Word. After showing me this, He spoke the most beautiful words to me I'd ever heard. He said, "There, Robin, is where we now walk in the cool of the evening."

I saw immediately the Scripture in Matthew 13:18-25 about the Parable of the Sower. Jesus spoke of the heart condition of man in that parable. The first heart was so hard that the light of Jesus just bounced off it, and it remained a dark desert wasteland. The second heart was able to absorb the light of Jesus, but the light was never seen by others. This heart continued to have much darkness. The third heart was the heart of one that received the light of Jesus but made a decision to pick and choose what would be reflected out to others. This heart was like a prism that refracted the light into a rainbow, but only part of the light could be seen. The last heart in the parable was transparent. This heart not only received the pure white light of Jesus but also allowed the pure white light (God's glory) to pass through it unchanged.

Of course, I would like to think that God's light is passing through me as it did in the last heart, but I know this is not always the case. This goal of a transparent heart is what I believe Paul wrote about in Philippians 3:13-14. We are to forget the past and press on to win the prize. That prize is to have the fullness of Christ's goodness and grace manifested in us and through us. I don't know how you feel, but I feel this is an exciting goal.

God Mail: Love Walk

This is God, and Jesus is Lord. You have seen a part of you that needs developed. Your love walk needs to be deepened a great deal before you can fully walk in the gifts of the Spirit that I have promised to you. Now that you understand that without a solid foundation, your temple will tumble, let us begin work on the foundation of your temple. (See I Corinthians 3:11-17)

Your temple must be firmly planted in the foundation of Jesus–His love. Without that rooting, it will make your temple flimsy and easily blown away. I tell you that you must develop a strong love walk with Me before any of what is promised will come to pass. I have been teaching you a great deal to get you to this point of understanding. You know that I have been guiding your understanding so that now you have enough knowledge for Me to work on you for greater works. I have been working on the ground to prepare your heart for seed. Now, we move on to the planting. I have seen the soil of your heart, and it is fertile and ready for planting.

I am glad you realize that love is what needs to be planted deep in your heart. Until now I had to show you that I really do love you. I love you and want the best for you. Now that you are truly convinced, it is time to plant My love deep in the fertile soil of your heart. When I plant My love in your heart, do you think anything other than My love can be harvested?

You know that when love is planted, the harvest will be love. How much of a love harvest you receive will be up to you. You must not let your heart be exposed to anything that will damage the crop. You must guard your heart. It is fragile soil too easily eroded by stormy weather. That is when you run to Me for protection and for strength. Come to Me, so I may fertilize your heart and make the soil capable of sustaining life to yield an overabundance of love.

I want to reveal My character to you. I want to answer the desire of your heart for a deeper love walk. I am pleased that you understand that without love all else is a fraud. (See I Corinthians 13) I know you want a real experience with Me–nothing superficial. You want people to know Me, and that is good. You want to tell people I can change lives. I know your heart. It is becoming less hardened. That shell of protection that you built around your heart is slowly being peeled off. Let Me be your protection so that you can be free to demonstrate My love to others. If they lash out to hurt you, let My armor protect you. It is no longer necessary for you to stand guard over your heart. I do that now. Let Me have all of you.

God Mail: The Heart, the Vine, and the Gardener

This is your Lord Jesus Christ, come to tell you of the heart in which I see. This heart is soft, pliable, and able to be shaped and molded as God would have it. That heart (once a desert wasteland–barren, with no vegetation) is now rich soil to plant and to grow the will of the Father. It is in the heart that desires of the Father are placed and there that they either grow or die on the vine. The vine is Jesus; the Gardener, the Caretaker, and the Nurturer is God. The Holy Spirit is there to guard the fruit. You see that the heart is seen by all the Trinity, and it is the heart that is seen alone. No longer do you have to be weighed down with worry about your behavior, for it is from the heart that your behavior will spring. It is from the heart that the mouth will speak. Do not fail to consider what you are becoming. Do not fail to consider what you have already become. You have grown, My child, and it is good to see the fruit of the Spirit flourish in the garden that the Lord has prepared in your heart.

So often the hearts of the children of God are barren. Their hearts do not flourish when they are unrepentant. Many Christians try to fix the outside without changing their heart issues. They strive to look the part of a Christian without letting the Gardener do the work. It is often the case that many play the roles set forth by man but fail to do what God requires. You see this with the Pharisees and Sadducees. They played the part of holy and sanctified but led no one to know the Lord and to understand His ways.

As for those who choose to let the Gardener plow the soil of their hearts and plant the seeds, they become discouraged at the requirements of relinquishing control. The seeds never have a chance to grow tall and strong. Growth is stunted to the degree of their unwillingness to change as the Father wills.

Next are those who become familiar enough with the Gardener to trust Him, and to allow growth. But they keep the fruit for themselves, and they do not share the wealth of the crop with others. Fear and trepidation control their willingness to share their wealth.

Finally, there are those who have come to the knowledge of the Gardener. They want the Gardener not only to have free reign over the gardens in their hearts but also to produce an abundance of fruit to be given to others—an overflow. (See Matthew 13:18-23) It is these fruit-bearers that much is given. To whom much is given, much is required....

God Mail: The Heart

This is your Lord and Savior, Jesus Christ. I am the anointed of God, and with the anointing comes all the power of God to do His will on earth as it is already done in heaven. You have a sense of My presence that many do not have, yet you still know that there is more to experience.

You asked that I search your heart and let Me have My way in that heart. (See Jeremiah 17:10) So when I search your heart, I find in that heart the habitat of God. It is in that heart that much will spring forth in the way of fruit to feed many. So you see, I am a God Who does search the heart of man, looking for a heart to inhabit. It is the Holy Spirit Who dwells in you, and as you have heard, He remodels the new abode. In the heart there is much to work with in the remodeling. The structure is already in place. The foundation is already poured, and the framework is already erected. Now it is time to begin the interior. Plans are laid out for the size of the rooms and the placements of such things as doors and windows. As the rooms begin to take shape, you will see that the walls, once built in order to protect yourself, are now being moved out to make more spacious rooms.

Just as it is in your physical home, so it is in your heart. When you first moved into your home, there were many rooms. The rooms were small, and the walls were put up haphazardly. There seemed to be no light. Closed-off rooms blocked the flow of air and travel through the house. Now, however, the house has been remodeled: walls torn down, rooms enlarged, and the flow of light and air no longer blocked.

So it is with your heart. If you ask Me to search your heart, I will and do. I will tell you what I see. I see a house most certainly under construction; the walls are being removed, and the light, airy rooms are taking shape. This is what the Father sees as He searches your heart. It is a house under construction, but it is the house (temple) of God. You would not have such a heart if you did not give Me access. Trust that your Father looks upon your heart and does not look upon your behavior. As you allow Him more access, you will see the outside of the temple (your behavior) also changed.

Right now your heart is looking better than your outside, but trust that this will not always be the case. I am yours, and you are Mine. That is how it is. Rejoice and be glad that the

Lord God Almighty looks upon your heart. It is a good heart. It is a heart under construction. (See Psalm 139:23) The construction is a continual process that will take a lifetime to complete. But be of great joy, for it is built on a solid foundation with everlasting effects. That is your joy. That is your promise. Now go and think on these things. Your Father has blessed you and has made you a blessing. Do not focus on the outside but focus on the heart that the Father sees. I tell you now it is a good heart with large breezy rooms where you can be free to live.

Chapter Four

I Say They Are There

So what does hardness of heart have to do with *not* hearing from God? The word "EVERYTHING" comes rushing to my mind! If your heart is hardened in a particular area, it will be difficult to receive what the Lord has for you in that area. How many times have you heard, "The baptism with the Holy Spirit is not for me," or "Healing passed away with the Early Church"? Without getting into a big theological discussion about these two topics, let me just say one thing about them. I read it in the Bible; I believed; I received. That's it; that's all!

I read in the Bible and also heard from many people about, "the gifts of the Spirit" (See I Corinthians 12:1-11). I had even seen a few believers operate in these gifts, and I wanted them. I knew, according to Acts 10:34, that God does not favor one believer over another, so I believed He would give them to me. I began to read everything I could about the gifts of the Spirit. I wanted them right now, and I meditated, pleaded, and cried out for God to give me these wonderful gifts. For the next four months that was all I could think about. Much of my prayer time I spent praying in tongues. Also, I believed the Lord would give me interpretation for my prayer language according to First Corinthians 14:13-14.

I sought God those four months for nothing else. Then one day it happened. I had already finished praying and was in my workout room when I just had to pray in tongues. It was nothing dramatic. I spoke in tongues, and then I spoke in English these words: "I say they are there, and they are there." Now talk about a hardened heart. I had prayed for the gifts for four months and finally heard, "I say they are there, and they are there." And can you believe it? I actually said, "What does that mean?" In the following week, God spoke these words to me two more times before I finally said, "Oh, He is telling me I have them!"

My husband, Bob, often comments about these eureka moments that we have with God and how God would react if He weren't filled with such patience and grace. Bob says that when God finally gets us to receive what He has given, He hits His forehead with the palm of His hand saying, "At last, they've got it!"

It is the hardness of heart that keeps us from believing that God has already given us all He has in Jesus Christ. The day we received Jesus into our hearts and our "spirit man" became born anew, we were given all things for godliness. Second Peter 1:3 (NIV) tells us, *"His divine power has given us everything we need for life and godliness through our knowledge of him who called us by his own glory and goodness."*

So there it is. It is that unbelieving heart in whatever area that keeps us from receiving. I have learned that if it is in His Word, believe it. Then, by the same measure of faith that He has given to every believer, ask for it, and receive it in the wonderful name of Jesus.

Chapter Five

God's Faithful Servant

I was not fortunate enough to grow up in a Word-based church. For the first 18 years of my life, I attended a mainline denominational church where I learned that God was pretty disgusted with me. I was just a rotten sinner that He could barely tolerate. It would have been unimaginable that He would want to talk with me. I believed that God was constantly judging me, and I was constantly failing Him. There was little discussion about salvation through Jesus Christ, but there was much discussion about hell.

By the time I was 18, I saw God as a mean, wrathful God that wanted to catch me doing something wrong, so He could zap me. I had an extremely large dose of guilt and condemnation that made me continually focus on my performance. I was paralyzed by perfectionism. It is no wonder that when I turned 18, I ran screaming from that church and from God. I wanted nothing to do with God, and I didn't until I was 40 years old.

Because God had been presented to me as harsh and hard, I could not understand when people told me about a God

Who was loving and caring. I began my adult life never considering God or attending church or living for Him. I lived my life pleasing myself. I was closed off from people who I perceived might harm me and relied solely on my first husband for the love I so desperately needed.

However, when your whole life is focused on one individual, it drains the life out of that person. I leaned so heavily on him for acceptance and for love that I killed any love he had for me. It is a heavy burden to be responsible for another's happiness. He was truly a wonderful person, but, without God in our lives, our relationship ended after 16 years. I can only imagine the tremendous weight that was lifted from him.

So at age 35, the center of who I was walked out the door, and I was left floundering for five years trying to figure out how to live. During those five years, I began to notice something strange. Repeatedly, I would encounter God in the most unusual places. One of the most bizarre encounters was in a bar. Yes, I said a bar!

One evening, while at a restaurant with co-workers, my ex-husband and his new wife came into the restaurant. I was determined to speak to them without any evidence that I was dying inside. After having a lovely conversation with them, I graciously turned, walked out of the restaurant, drove to a bar, and proceeded to mourn over a lost love. Oh, I was pitiful. I sat by myself determined to make myself feel every awful emotion.

I wasn't paying much attention to people coming or going, but I did notice one gentlemen come into the bar. He looked my way, and I quickly dropped my eyes down towards my drink. Before long, he plopped himself down beside me, and I immediately thought the worst. I found myself getting a little angry with him. I just wanted to be left alone–not really.

He started to tell me how strange it was for him to be in this place. He really needed to be in Pittsburgh at a business meeting, but he just had to stop. I thought to myself, he must have a drinking problem. But that was not the case. He explained that God had told him to stop and talk with someone. He had no idea who that someone was, but he thought it might be me. We spent an hour together talking about God. Then just as quickly as he came in, he left.

I realized after he left that I felt great. The terrible anxiety and sorrowful feelings I had were gone. I didn't realize at the time, but I had just had an encounter with God through one of His faithful servants. God was already speaking to me. It would be just a few months later that I would have another encounter with God that would change my life forever.

God Mail: He Is the Potter

This is your Lord and Savior, Jesus Christ. I am here with you in spirit and in truth to tell you things of the hidden heart. You long to be perfected in your walk with God. This is your desire: that somehow while here on the earth, you can become the perfected image of Jesus Christ. You know in your head that this is not possible, for in this life on earth sin abounds. This is not to discourage but to bring expectations of perfection into more of a reality so that you will be able to live with joy. You will not be perfected here on earth into the exact perfect image of Jesus. Rather it is the hope of glory to which you seek. (See Colossians 1:27)

The hope of glory is what all God's children seek. It is being made perfect that you are seeking. You seek to know better the One Who created you, and you seek to be accepted by Him for who you are. But when you think on who you are, you must focus on who you are through the One Who died for you and redeemed you. I am the way that made it possible for the Father to see you perfect. I am the way in which you were perfected. But you will battle with the flesh until you are either caught up in the sky with Me or meet death and the resurrection. It is not until then that your body, soul, and spirit are joined together in the perfection that you seek. So what are you to do while on the earth?

You will trust that I will be with you every step of the way–guiding you into the light and further delivering you from darkness. As long as you continue to seek after perfection, you put demands on others for perfection, and your love walk is affected. I am the One Who will deliver you from evil and from the wiles of the devil. The devil understands this is an area you are weak. You are weakened by the sense of chastisement and condemnation every time you feel you are wrong or not perfect. (See Romans 8:1) This perfection is Mine not yours. You are free to be who you are right now. Yes, you can trust that I am changing you from glory to glory, but it is My glory, not yours, that you receive.

Do not condemn yourself because of your weakness, but focus on the promises of God. As you seek after My kingdom and My righteousness, then all will be given that is promised. (See Matthew 6:33) The promised land that you seek is there now. You can be in the land right now. I have cleared the way for you to enter in now. You can enter now while on your way to being perfected. But *the being* is now. *Being* what God intended is a process slowed by focusing on what you think you are to be and what you think you are not to be. You heard today that My grace is given to you so that nothing you do right or wrong makes you any more or less able. I make you able. I am the One Who gives. I give, and you receive. You just are and receive.

You really are much like the vessel you imagine when you sing to Me of being shaped and molded. You are just the earth. Until I begin My work in you, you are without form and purpose. But when you receive Me into your heart, your spirit, then that spirit made perfect is the blueprint to which the earthen lump of clay begins to conform. (See II Corinthians 4:7) Your flesh, the lump of clay, becomes molded and shaped to receive the purposes of God Almighty. That lump of clay, once without form and function, becomes what God intended. (See Isaiah 64:8, Romans 9:21) You no longer are responsible for the work that needs to be done. You are only the recipient of the work that is done in you and through you. Your *being* is to only be what God fills you with. If He sovereignly fills you with works of a prophet, you are only *being* that. If He fills you full with teaching of His Word, you become that. *Being* what He has made you. You see how this is.

You are on My potter's wheel, as I will you to be what I make you. Your work is just to receive, and be what I have made you.... Just let Me fill you with what I have made you to be. Receive it, and just be, as I will, not as you will. As it is My will for you, so be it.

God Mail: My Now Identity

This is your God in heaven and your Jesus, Lord of your everything—here today with you as you come to Me. I want to say certain things to you that you fear are not of Me but of you. I tell you now that it is possible to please your Father in heaven and have Him tell you of His pleasure without fearing pride. How can I show you that you are pleasing? How can I tell you of the joy I have for you without pride entering into your heart? I can tell you because I guard your heart. You can receive My loving words without thinking you are the one saying these things out of pride. I tell you I have not given you a spirit of fear, so you are free to receive from your Father messages that exalt without fear. (See II Timothy 1:7)

You for so long received criticism, and, as a result, you tried to become perfect. Perfection had you bound up so tightly. I tell you, you have been made perfect by My Son, and you are accepted. (See Colossians 1:28) Now you receive My correction, but often you reject My praise. I tell you I can praise you without your fearing that this is wrong.

How can I let you know that you are pleasing and that you bring joy? My children are not to feel that I am angry with them. I want them to know I see them as perfect, and I love them unconditionally. Begin to see yourself as a joy to your God–not by what you say, think, or feel but because I have given you all things for life and godliness. (See II Peter 1:23)

You are a joy to Me. How I love to hear your voice in the morning. I love to hear you call out to your Father. Do you think it is only you who can call out to Me statements of love and devotion? (See Ephesians 3:17-19) I am faithful, loving, good, and kind, but you fail to see Me as you long to be. I put My Spirit in you along with the fruit of My Spirit. The love I have for you is in you. So does it not make sense that I would tell My image of the love and the joy and the happiness you bring to Me?

You seek Me every day, and that gives Me great joy. I tell you this for encouragement, not to bring the sin of pride on you. Fear not, for the God of your everything protects, guides, and loves you. You are a joy. You follow after My heart. You are a joy. Begin to see yourself as that. Don't always see yourself as incomplete and without virtue. You are in a process, but I see you complete and whole. I want you to see yourself that way.

Criticism in your early years was a way of life for you. Now see praise and joy and peace as your constant companions as you walk with Me. I bring those to you. Receive them, and praise Me. You are My likeness. Do you think it is pleasing to see My likeness condemning herself? See yourself as the likeness of Christ.

Last night you told others they must begin to see themselves differently. You say these things with conviction. Now live it. See yourself as I do. Believe you are acceptable and pleasing to your Heavenly Father. I look at you as I look at My Son. So pleasing is My Son. So pleasing is My Son's likeness in you. I love you. Walk with Me.

Chapter Six

A Living Testament

As I said before, I had hardened my heart to God. I thought He only wanted to hurt me and make me feel rotten. However, the more my life spiraled out of control, the more desperate I became. I even started to listen to people when they would talk to me about Jesus. However, there was still a need in me to solve my own problems. By the time I got so desperate to trust God and to receive Jesus, I was seeing a psychiatrist, a psychologist, and also participating in group counseling. I was told I was depressed and was prescribed higher and higher doses of Prozac. Needless to say, I was lost.

Then someone entered my life that presented God in a way that made me seriously consider what I called "this God thing." It was my brother's wife, Blanky. She is a spirit-filled Latin from South America. I had never met anyone like her, and, to be perfectly honest, she was peculiar. (Deuteronomy 14: 2 [Amp] ... *"and the Lord has chosen you to be a peculiar people to Himself, above all the nations on the earth."*) The way she thought, spoke, and acted was strange. No one in his or her right mind can think about, talk about, and praise God constantly. But there she was. The joy of the Lord flowed out of her, and I became intrigued.

I spent two weeks with this woman while visiting my brother, Tim, in Florida. I fell in love with her. The life of Christ was so apparent in her that for the first time in my life I wanted to know the God she was telling me she knew. Her life was a living testament to the love of God. She spoke to me about all the wonderful ways in which God had blessed her life. We talked for hours about God without growing tired. By the end of the two weeks, she asked if I would receive Jesus as my Lord. But there was still hardness in my heart that made me unable to commit to Him. I said I would not be a hypocrite like those I saw in the church I grew up in so many years before. I saw too many professing Christians behave in such ungodly ways that I couldn't commit to God unless I really knew He was for real.

Before I left she told me that she asked God to send me a godly man. I had been dating unsuccessfully for years. Now if you know anything about true believers in God's Word, you know that her prayer was answered immediately. (Matthew 21:22 [Amp] *"And whatever you ask for in prayer, having faith and [really] believing, you will receive."*)

When I arrived home, I immediately began attending a motorcycle safety course. I was about to turn 40 years of age and wanted to do something to memorialize the occasion. What better thing to do as a depressed 40-year-old woman all alone in the world than to learn how to careen down the highway on a motorized two-wheeled vehicle?

Can you guess what happened? I met that Christian man my little spirit-filled Christian sister-in-law asked God to send to me. I later learned about the term prayer warrior. Whether that is an acceptable term in most segments of the Christian population, I don't know. All I know is that she believed the Word, made her requests known to God, and received. Do you see who helped shape my Christian walk? Praise the Lord for sending me someone who knew Him intimately and was not afraid to testify of His great goodness!

God Mail: Prayer

This is God, and Jesus is Lord. You are here with Me today, and the joy of the Lord is upon you. You can resist the enemy and submit your all to Me. (See James 4:7) It is possible through the power of the Holy Spirit to live this life upright with God. Trust that I have a good plan for you and live in the knowledge that God is love. He will never harm you.

It is right to pray for friends and neighbors. All prayer prayed in the will of your Heavenly Father is good and acceptable. Continue in those prayers: not just for family but for whole neighborhoods. Prayers are powerful and can change situations. Trust it is not wasted time.

You prayed for the peace and the joy and the love of your God to fall in your house this Thanksgiving as your family gathers together. It is acceptable that this prayer be prayed. You can trust that your God wants to fill every home with the love that surpasses knowledge. It is your prayer time that changes the very atmosphere on earth.

Prayer is the place in which hopes and dreams for a better life are created. It is the will of the Father that His children come to Him in prayer to establish and ground themselves in Him, Almighty God. You have learned that it is a vital part of becoming more like the Son. You must make a commitment to commune with God each morning. Prayer is vital to your walk with God. (See James 5:16) Know that anytime you come in prayer, your life is transformed. Transformation may be great or small, but it is necessary to your walk. Come as you are, and I, your Almighty God, will show you a better way, a more perfect way to live. So pray without ceasing for those neighbors, friends, loved ones.... See those prayers become manifested on earth as it is in heaven.

Love is the key to coming closer, and prayer is the lock in which the key is turned. (See Galatians 5:6) I am the door in which to walk through to the other side where all the blessings lie. See your reality as I do. See the only true God as your only hope, joy, and love. All other things you think will bring those blessings are deception.

Chapter Seven

God Has A Plan

I was about to embark on something totally outside of my understanding–learning how to ride a motorcycle. However, God had a plan that not only included motorcycles but a new life with Him.

I was totally fearless about riding a motorcycle even though I had never operated one. I found that I had the ability to ride a motorcycle successfully and to pass with a pretty good score. However, I credited my success to one instructor, Bob Joyce.

For two weeks Bob was extremely encouraging and patient with all the students. He had a quiet, calm demeanor that put everyone at ease. Learning a new skill at the age of 40 was not easy, but he helped to make it fun.

After I passed the test, I impulsively ran over to Bob, threw my arms around him, and thanked him for all his hard work. Then out of my mouth flew these words, "Let's go riding sometime."

To my surprise, he answered back with a big grin, "Sure, anytime."

It wasn't until two months later that we went on that ride. During those two months, we talked on the phone, and the conversations, more often than not, were about God. He told me he was a Christian, and he asked me if I was one. My response was odd. Rather than answer his question, I told him about my experience with my sister-in-law, Blanky. Shortly after that, we met to ride motorcycles.

I had just bought my first motorcycle, and I was absolutely thrilled to be riding it with anyone. At this point, I just saw Bob as a riding buddy. We rode for a few hours, but when we came back to my house, we talked about God well into the evening. I asked many questions, and his answers were amazingly thoughtful and easy to understand. He was presenting God in much the same way as Blanky did. I started to believe that God was possibly more about love than I had been shown as a child. I noticed that Bob and Blanky had similar experiences with God that showed His great love and faithfulness. But still, I was skeptical.

Shortly after our first ride, Bob invited me to his church. When I went, it was much like the lively church service I had attended with Blanky and Tim in Florida. The songs were wonderful, but what struck me the most was how I felt. I had never gone to church where I could feel the presence of the Lord. Of course, I didn't understand what I was experiencing at the time. I just knew at the end of each service, I was in tears.

Later, I came to understand this was the Spirit of the Living God ministering to my hard heart. What fascinated me the most was how the Spirit manifested Himself in me. I had a physical feeling that my heart was being squeezed. What made this even stranger was that this physical manifestation closely resembled the feelings I would experience when I was suffering from panic attacks. However, I could tell it was not the same thing. This similar experience made it easy for me later to understand the Scriptures that related to Satan being a copycat. He mimics the truth, but praise God for His Word and His Spirit that gives believers discernment. Second Corinthians 11:14 and First Corinthians 2:14 [NIV] state,

> *And no wonder, for Satan himself masquerades as an angel of light.... The man without the Spirit does not accept the things that come from the Spirit of God, for they are foolishness to him, and he cannot understand them, because they are spiritually discerned.*

Chapter Eight

Find My Socks!

Bob and I occasionally saw each other for the next two months. Each time we met, we would talk about God. I remember one time we planned to go shopping. We had our coats on ready to leave the house, but, once again, we started a discussion about God. An hour later we were still in the living room in our coats talking about God.

We did go shopping that day. I complained to Bob that my brother, Alan, who had just moved out of my house to take a new job in Florida, must have accidentally packed my winter socks. I decided to buy more that day, not understanding the significance of those lost socks.

We arrived back at my home late and continued our earlier discussion about God. I finally got frustrated with the conversation. Bob simply told me to pray, and God would reveal Himself to me, as if God had not done so already. However, with a hardened heart you truly are blinded and cannot see the things of God. Second Corinthians 4:4 (Amp) actually explains this condition.

> *For the god of this world has blinded the unbelievers'*
> *minds [that they should not discern the truth],*
> *preventing them from seeing the illuminating light*
> *of the Gospel of the glory of Christ (the Messiah),*
> *Who is the Image and Likeness of God.*

I immediately took issue with prayer. I said, "Pray to what? It's just air to me."

Bob very patiently and quietly said, "Try it; pray for those socks you can't find. He will show you that He is for real."

Well, I love a challenge, so in my most sarcastic voice I said, "Okay, God! If you are for real, find my socks!" The topic of God ended, and, at one in the morning, Bob went home.

As I turned off the lights downstairs and began to walk upstairs to bed, I thought about my socks. It came to me out of nowhere, "Look in the closet in the spare bedroom." I had already looked there and was about to dismiss the thought, but I remembered my prayer about those lost socks. I believe this was the moment that God's faith, which He has given to every person, rose up in my spirit, and I grabbed hold of the promise that He would reveal Himself to me personally.

With an expectancy I never placed on God before, I went to that closet. I opened the door and looked in hoping to see those socks. To my utter amazement and unspeakable joy, there were the winter socks I had prayed to God to find for me. I met God in, of all places, that closet as I stared at those socks. I know I had looked there before but never saw them. I know I had looked for God before but never saw Him until that night when He opened my blind eyes to see.

I ran to the phone knowing that Bob could not possibly be home yet. I left a message on his machine. I simply said between all my laughter, "I found my socks." I didn't find out until the next day that Bob was expecting that phone call. He had prayed to the Father all the way home to answer my little prayer for my socks so that I would know God was for real. Bob told me that when he got home, he went right to the answering machine. Before he hit the button to listen to the message, he knew in his heart that it was me.

Praise to God! God revealed to me that night His promise from Psalm 103:8 (Amp): *"The Lord is merciful and gracious, slow to anger and plenteous in mercy and loving-kindness."* That night was the start of my relationship and fellowship with God through Jesus Christ, His Son.

Chapter Nine

Salvation

I can't tell you the day or the hour that Jesus Christ came into my heart. I believe it was the night I met God in the closet of my spare bedroom. After that night, I became hungry and thirsty for God. I wanted to know this God Who gave me spiritual eyes to see Him that night. I started to go to church with Bob more often to try to learn about this God, Who I was told loved me unconditionally.

One morning while getting ready for church, just a few weeks after my experience in the closet, I heard, "You're pregnant." I said to myself, "What a stupid thought." Having had a hysterectomy at age 34, I was completely bewildered by the thought of being pregnant.

I went to church that day with a sense that something had changed in me. I sat beside Bob and listened to a wonderful man of God deliver a message God had prepared my heart to receive. As I was sitting there, I felt a strange sensation of burning in my toes. That burning sensation began to flow up my legs, travel through my torso, and radiate out to my fingertips. It stopped at my neck, and the familiar squeezing of my heart began.

I began to panic and told Bob what was happening. He asked if I wanted to leave, but something had me glued to the pew. At one point the congregation was asked to stand, and I had no idea if my legs would hold me. I did get to my feet, but I felt so strange that I just concentrated on breathing. We sat back down, and I tried to remain as calm as I could.

At this point, my experience with altar calls was limited. I had been asked in Florida to go forward to publicly confess Jesus as my Lord and Savior and receive His salvation. I could not bring myself to do that. Doing anything publicly was an extremely traumatic affair. So the thought of standing in front of people I didn't know to receive Jesus Christ into my heart struck terror into me.

Thank God for a pastor who followed the leading of the Holy Spirit. This gentle man of God simply and quietly gave a salvation message on the love of God and on the acceptance of Jesus as our personal Savior. Then he led the entire congregation in the Sinner's prayer for salvation.

I prayed that prayer with a conviction I had never had about anything. I found once again that I was reduced to tears. The burning sensation left, but the squeezing of my heart continued. In fact, I am experiencing it right now as I put these words on paper. I now know this sensation as the Holy Spirit's way of assuring me of His indwelling presence in my heart.

If you have never received the Lord Jesus as your personal Savior, it is just as simple, albeit, miraculous as John 3:16 (Amp) says,

> *For God so greatly loved and dearly prized the world that He [even] gave up His only begotten (unique) Son, so that whoever believes in (trusts in, clings to, relies on) Him shall not perish (come to destruction, be lost) but have eternal (everlasting) life.*

If you sincerely believe John 3:16, then pray this prayer of salvation right now.

> *Father, of my Lord Jesus Christ, I have sinned against you. I didn't understand this before because I didn't know you. But now you have introduced yourself to me, and I believe you are the One and Only Living God. I understand that you sent Jesus here to earth to die for my sins, and, in that one great act of love, my sins were forever and always washed away. I am sure that Jesus paid for all my sins, even the ones that I will do from this day forward. But because I believe that your Almighty power raised Jesus Christ from the dead making Him spiritually alive again, I also believe that same power has raised my spirit from the dead. I now ask by faith that Jesus comes into my heart to live. I commit my life to you through Jesus*

> *Christ. I thank you now, Father, for my new life in Christ. I know I will forever be your child, and I will profess Jesus as my Lord and Savior.*

If you prayed this prayer from your heart, I want to be the first to welcome you into your new family. You are now a brother or a sister in Christ. Praise the Lord!

God Mail: Glory, Grace, and Mercy

This is your Lord and Savior, Jesus. I am with you today and every day. This is the voice of the Lord that you hear. I speak today of glory, grace, and mercy. It is the grace and mercy of God that you received upon salvation. It is His grace and mercy that He continues to give in abundance.

Let us first have a clear understanding of what is meant by grace and mercy. Grace is something that is given. Grace is never deserved by the one receiving it, so there can be no bragging about earning it. It is a free gift given without any exchange. It is just received. Mercy, on the other hand, relates to something that is withheld. What is withheld is God's wrath. His wrath is withheld by the blood of Jesus. Mercy is extended to believers once they receive redemption by the grace of God. The grace is Jesus Christ given as a free gift, and God's mercy is extended because of Jesus.

God's wrath was poured out upon Jesus instead of sinners. So you see that by grace you were saved, and by mercy you were not given what you deserved. You were given grace (Jesus), the unmerited favor of God—undeserved and unearned. You were given God's mercy by this grace (Jesus). They go hand-in-hand; grace always precedes God's mercy. And what made God extend grace and mercy to man that sinned against God? It was God's glory. (See Exodus 34:6-7) It is God's love that caused God the Father to sacrifice God the Son. It is glory (God's nature) that caused Him to do this for man that He made in His image. Man was the very glory of God because man was created in the image and likeness of God. God put Himself, His glory, in man. So when man fell due to sin, the glory left him. No longer was man clothed in the glory. When Moses was in the very presence of God, glory was upon him. But when Moses was out of the presence of God, the glory left him. (See Exodus 34:29-35, II Corinthians 3:6-18)

Glory (God's attributes and character), grace (God's gift of favor and blessings undeserved and unearned–Jesus), and mercy (God's willingness to forgive) are all necessary for salvation.

Salvation is not just receiving Jesus (grace), but it is coming back to the very likeness of God. That is why you develop from glory to glory. Adam had been given all that God possessed. He was given full knowledge, understanding, and power to rule and to reign for God on this earth. He was quite literally God of this world. Once the glory was gone from Adam, God was motivated by His own nature and attributes to extend grace and mercy to man. It was His plan to bring man back to the original glory he once possessed. All three must work together to cause this to come to pass.

This is why it is so important for God's children to remember who they are in Jesus Christ. If they do not, they forget who they are becoming–the very likeness of God (glory restored). So if you forget who you are in Christ Jesus, you also forget about God's grace and loving mercy. It is Who I AM. I AM love! Love is what causes this all to be. I created out of love, and it is love that will restore. This is what I have to say to you today. Do not forget who you are in Christ Jesus. It is this knowledge that will sustain you forever. Glory, grace, and mercy go hand-in-hand, but they are only received through your position in Jesus Christ. Where are you? (See Ephesians 2:4-10)

God Mail: Eternal Salvation

You asked Me what could cause such differing views on salvation, and I will tell you. You know, of course, that I will raise the name Jesus above all others as Lord and Savior.

You are confused as to how so many find it easy to accept that I would punish disobedience with lack of entrance into heaven. So many believe I would be a Father Who would turn My back on My children. They believe I am not capable of loving enough to keep My hand on My children.

I am a God of the impossible. As unruly as My children can be, there was One Who did it all–even for them. What so many fail to realize is that I sent the One Who could stay in the Father's perfect will, and it is because of His work that all thereafter can rest in it.

I spoke of two views concerning salvation. One is God-centered, and the other is self-centered. The God-centered view allows you to seek Me because you believe that My Son did it all. (See II Corinthians 5:17-21) The self-centered view causes you to continue to see through the eyes of a sinner, forgetting that My grace and mercy are enough. You have heard both before, but you struggle to understand how so many can choose the latter view. In many instances you see through sinner's eyes, but your seeking after My ways is delivering you over to the God-centered view. However, not all have found their way out of this self-centered view; therefore, they choose to torture themselves with thoughts of lost salvation. (See John 6:37)

I do not want My children thinking that I am a Father Who haphazardly loses children here and there as an uncaring father of the world might do. (See John 10:27-30) I want all of God's children to see Me as their God—as their Father—loving enough to keep all My children safely tucked in My arms. Now, as with small children, discipline and life-experiences are necessary to help them grow, but they are never allowed to just wander away from Me.

God Mail: Eternity–Everlasting Life

This is your Lord and Savior, Jesus. I am your Christ, the Anointed. You see how the world comes in on your thoughts and causes you to see things in a confused way. It is the wavering that causes you to struggle in prayer at times. You let the viewpoint of man cloud what you have learned through My Word and through revelation. I am your source of truth. In the Word you see My truth, and when the Holy Spirit reveals it to you, it is yours forever. (See James 1:5-8)

Salvation

The world needs to know that I am a faithful, loving God. It is Mine to keep My children safe. You cannot in your own power keep yourself. It is fruitless to try. But with Me, I have promised that I will never leave you or forsake you. (See Hebrews 13:5) I am yours forever, and you are Mine. Let us rest on this and move on to other more pressing concerns. To constantly revisit salvation with doubt is of the devil and is not My will for My children. I have the power to save as you call upon Me to do so. You called out for Jesus, and, as a result, you were born into the kingdom of God. (See John 3:1-8) You are no longer a child of Satan but a child of your ever-present, all-knowing, all-powerful God. That means there is now no more condemnation. You are Mine forever. Do not continue to let people sway you. It is as I have told you. You do not pass in and out of eternity. Hear this and let it be settled.

Look at the great friends of God such as Abraham. Did he do perfectly after I established My covenant with him? No. Did I threaten to remove Myself from him? No. I was faithful to the promise even when he was not. This is how it is. I am faithful to do My will and to fulfill My promises.

Earthen vessels are limited, but God is all in all and is more than enough to keep His promises. Yes, men exercise free will, but once you are in My covenant of grace, you are eternal and are never separated from Me. That is how it must be, or you would not be able to trust Me. So many use the excuse that it is their choices that cause lost redemption. But nothing they could ever do would cause the incorruptible seed (See I Peter 1:23) to be removed once placed in their hearts. That is how it must be, or Satan could kill My children. I am speaking spiritually not physically. Yes, Satan has caused many of My children to die due to lack of knowledge or has rendered them ineffective in the kingdom of God. But separating My children from Me is not possible. Once you have the incorruptible, it is exactly that–incorruptible. You will not perish but will have everlasting life. Now stand on that promise and move on to more abundance.

God Mail: Transformation through His Spirit

This is your Lord and Savior, Jesus Christ. It is in the name of Jesus that you are able to cast out demons. (See Mark 16:17-18) In the name of Jesus, you place your hopes. Those hopes of glory come from the Father and manifest themselves in the form of changed behavior. You see your behavior changed from glory to glory, but, occasionally, you see yourself as you once were. It is a hard lesson for those who once were children of the devil to see themselves changed into the children of God. (See Romans 8:14-15) Often this is the case with many of God's children. The gift of salvation is so awe-inspiring and complete in its transforming abilities, yet many do not accept it without thinking somehow they must add to it.... (See Galatians 3:3) Sealed forever by the Spirit, it is through the ministry of the Holy Spirit that this transformation is complete and being made complete.

There are two separate transformations. The transformation upon salvation is already done (See Hebrews 10:14-23), but the other one is ongoing. (See Romans 12:1-2) All fall short of God's glory, but, through the mighty workings of the blood sacrifice of the Son of God, Jesus, all who believe and receive are glorified. This causes confusion for many.

Some think that they should be able to be perfect now, not recognizing the two separate events. Others believe they can do what only Jesus can do and try to perfect themselves. This also is wrong thinking. Still others accept the truth, yet they often find themselves striving for perfection in their own effort. However, for those who can just believe and receive from the Father, there is great joy and peace.

I would have all My children believe the latter and just believe, receive, and rest in the peace that this brings. Do what I tell you to do, and be what I tell you to be. No, you are not to be a robot ordered mindlessly about, but you are to be My child wanting to serve a sovereign God and obey out of love and respect for God the Father. You can do this if you trust in a God you see as all-knowing, loving, and faithful. See how it is? If you are trusting in a God you see this way, then it is easy to believe and to receive. But if you are serving out of self-motives or out of fear or due to a religious spirit, then your serving is not joyful, and life is difficult. Meditate on the God of love. Put your hope in Jesus. Trust that His Spirit leads you and guides you into all truth.

God Mail: The Seed

This is your Lord and Savior, Jesus Christ. This is concerning the authority you have through Jesus. Jesus died for the sins of the world. That is why He died for all of mankind. But for those who actually accept His work on the cross and receive the resurrected life of Jesus, they become the God-kind. You know that like begets like. So it is with spiritual things as well.

When Jesus came and gave His life, He knew that not all would share in the gift of salvation. (See Ephesians 2:8) Some would hear the Word and be unchanged. But others would hear the Word about salvation and accept it with open hearts and minds. To the latter, it is the resurrection that should take hold of them and cause them to change into that to which they were born. You saw that Jesus first came to the world through the womb of a woman. (See John 10:1-2) He became sin and conquered mightily in order to be the spiritual womb through which all mankind must pass through to become God-kind. (See John 10:9) Many have passed through the spiritual womb of Jesus but have not learned what they have become. They have become spiritual babies, but, without knowledge, they never grow into the likeness of the Father, the Son, and the Holy Spirit as it is designed. So they return to the world in which they came, aborting the *hope* of salvation–a spiritual abortion.

It is to this I will speak. No, this does not mean lost salvation. This means that the pregnancy of hope, peace, joy, love and all the fruit gets cast aside. The pregnancy of the perfect will and plan of God (See Jeremiah 29:11) for their lives gets cast out–the seed never nourished is never allow to grow. The embryo of the seed is never allowed to break forth and take root. The embryo is never allowed to release the energy stored inside. It is overshadowed once again by the dark. This does not mean that the seed does not still exist but that it is never allowed to flourish.

The purpose of the message is to show you that without nourishment from the Word and the Spirit, My spiritual babies stay spiritual babies, even with the seed of hope, peace, joy, love, and all the fruit hidden in their hearts. Some do not even recognize that it lies dormant within them. Time to wake the seed within My spiritual babies. Time to send those willing to do the work for the kingdom of God. I am that seed planted in them but overshadowed by the darkness of the world. For those willing, it is time to cast light on those seeds and tend to the gardens that will grow in their hearts. It is time. Go and see the harvest time about to begin.

Chapter Eleven

Slow Down!

Bob and I married only nine months after meeting. Most people were genuinely happy for us. Bob had been walking with the Lord for many years; however, it was an up-and-down relationship. In desperate times, he would rely totally on God, but, in other times, he would do for himself.

Before Bob met me, he cast his care for finding a wife upon God. He did not date for five years. Instead, he threw himself into his work, family, and church. Much of his spare time was spent in church, and he believed that was where he would meet the wife God had for him. Little did he know, his future wife would be found in a motorcycle safety course. Since then, both of us have learned that you cannot put God in a box. In Isaiah 55:8-9 (Amp), God clearly tells us:

> *For My thoughts are not your thoughts, neither are your ways My ways, says the Lord. For as the heavens are higher than the earth, so are My ways higher than your ways and My thoughts than your thoughts.*

So there I was—a vision of loveliness, whizzing around the motorcycle course, and the first words my future husband said to me were, "Slow down!" Later, we would hear those words from many people when we told them of our plans to marry. However, that didn't slow us down. We knew in our spirits that God wanted us to be together, so we charged ahead. We quickly found out that when you step out before God's timing, the path is hard.

The first year of our marriage was very difficult. We had rushed out ahead of God by marrying so quickly. I was not prepared for all that was required of me in this brand-new life with God and with a new husband. Bob and I knew in our hearts that God wanted us to be together, but I did not know how to be a godly wife. I was rebellious to God and to Bob.

Throughout my adult life, I had experienced difficulty with authority. I had my way of thinking and acting. I did what I wanted to do, when I wanted to do it. Initially, anytime God or Bob tried to rein me in, I was like a wild colt. I bucked and kicked and fussed and fumed, trying to get my own way. It was not pretty. Did I mention that I had married a man who knew how to get on his knees and pray?

It would be months before I settled down and accepted that I could not continue this way. I was going to ruin another marriage, as well as any hope of becoming more acquainted with God. But as I studied more of God's Word and learned more about the love of God, I began to yield (submit) to the prompting (the still quiet voice) of the Holy Spirit.

God Mail: God's Beast of Burden

This is your Lord and Savior, Jesus Christ. It is a desire of yours to know the One you serve. Your desire is not unlike so many that come to the cross. It is at the cross that many find salvation, and at the cross that a journey begins. Unfortunately, many stop at the cross of salvation and go no further than receiving the promise of eternal life. But there are those who see beyond the initial salvation experience and let Me have My way in their hearts. They have the revelation that there is much more the Father needs. He has need of you.

So, as not to offend, I will first tell you that I love you, and I see you as more than a beast of burden. But, for this lesson, I will use the example of the donkey needed for the triumphant ride of your Savior. (See Luke 19:30-31) I tell you there is more to that story. The young colt can be seen as a fresh new life upon salvation. Jesus triumphantly wins the heart of a new child of God. Jesus rides upon the newly born in victory and in truth–guiding and directing. There is little resistance, and the colt knows the gentleness of the One Who has become His master. But, eventually, the colt begins to grow and to learn. What is learned does not always cause obedience but rebellion. The beast begins to think higher thoughts of himself than he ought. The beast is no longer the beast of burden to do the work of God Almighty but has his own will and desires. This is a beast of burden that can no longer be used.

The child of God can be seen much the same way. I am your guide, and I steer you in the direction you can best be used in the kingdom of God. But sometimes, in your own wisdom, you think you can guide yourself. (See Isaiah 55:8-9, Proverbs 3:5-8) You are Mine. You have a desire to be used, and you also know the Lord has need of you. I will get done what is needed to be done here on earth as it is in heaven. I am able. I will work through you and others willing to yield. But it is yours to yield.

You have asked for the good and perfect will of God to be done in you and through you. You are really asking that you be My beast of burden. Just as the farmer uses the beast of the field to sow and gather, so too does your God use you. So when I say beast of burden, that is what is meant. You do not have to figure out how I will do through you what I have planned. Yours is to yield and be obedient. A farmer does not ask advice from his beast; he does not rely on the wisdom of the beast; he only relies on the beast's ability to be used. He keeps the beast and does his best for the beast because that is his responsibility.

I am your God Who loves you and cares for you. Yes, I will use you. Your responsibility is to be available. But because of the great love I have for you, I would do all for you. It is My love for you that will cause your desires to be like Mine. Ask Me for My wisdom, knowledge, and understanding, and do not rely on yours. Ask Me to be your all sufficient One. Just as the beast relies on the farmer to supply all its needs, I will do the same for you. I am your head (mind, eyes, ears, and mouth included). You are the body to do My will. I have need of you. Stay that little colt–fresh as the day of salvation. Let Me have My way in you. You will see that I can do all through you.

Chapter Twelve

To Know About Each Other

Part of being a godly wife was learning to submit to my husband. It said it right there in the Bible. But every time I read Scripture about the responsibilities to God and to my husband that word "submit" would make my skin crawl. I would feel anger and fear rise up in me. How could I obey the Word of God in this area?

The Scriptures concerning submission are found in Ephesians 5:22 and James 4:7. In the first Scripture I was told to submit to my husband, and, in the second, I was told to submit to God. My concepts of submission, humility, and meekness were so distorted that it was hard for me to understand what God meant by these words. Not until I moved from a relationship into a deep fellowship with God and with Bob did I begin to understand what these words truly meant.

Because Bob and I had rushed into marriage so quickly, it did not take us long to realize that we did not know one another. In the nine months before our marriage, we came to *know about* each other through the telling of our life stories.

However, until we lived with one another day in and day out, we didn't really *know* each other.

I began to realize that my relationship with Bob and my relationship with God were similar. I had established a relationship with Bob through marriage and with God through the blood of Jesus. However, I did not know either of them intimately because there was not enough fellowship (spending quality time with them so that intimacy and trust could grow).

When you date, you have a relationship with that person. But when you marry, the fact that you are together with little separation should cause you to become closer and more intimate with that person (fellowship). With fellowship comes more trust in and reliance on that person. You allow that person more intimate access to you.

At the beginning I did not have fellowship with God or with Bob. So every time the word "submit" was mentioned through sermons or reading God's Word, I continued to be rebellious. Not until God and Bob helped me to relearn what love truly meant according to God's Word did I begin to understand the true meaning of submission. That reeducation only came through much time spent with both God and Bob.

Only after my mind was renewed through this fellowship time did I come to understand love as an action, not an emotion. All my life I vowed that I would do only what someone else was willing to do for me (an equal exchange). It did not take me long to realize that my way was not God's way. What I thought was love for so many years was only lust and gratification of my selfish desires. I learned that God's way of loving is the ability to act lovingly even when there is no hope of a fair exchange.

I recall the first time I had to do something loving and kind when all my emotions were saying to do the opposite. Bob and I had a huge argument, and I knew I was right. My plan of action was to pout and fume until he admitted he was wrong and saw the light according to Robin. I went to God in prayer, petitioning the Lord to show Bob the error of his ways. God's response both shocked and amazed me. God showed me that I might be part of the problem, but even if I was not, what victory was there in making Bob feel wrong and humiliated. I knew that I was to go to Bob and apologize. (Apologizing was something new for me, especially if I thought I was right.) But, at this point, I had a greater hunger for love and peace in my marriage.

I went to Bob and apologized, and, to my amazement, he apologized to me, too. I can't even remember why we argued. All I know is that the terrible feelings went away immediately. Instead of hanging on to the anger and the hurt, we spent the day enjoying each other. That was God's love–an action not an emotion. That was submitting myself unto the Lord and to my husband, trusting in their love for me. You cannot submit until you know the love of God. Praise God that He gave me a husband that understood how to love me God's way. Believe me, he got to practice it a great deal the first year of our marriage.

God Mail: Hidden Pride

This is God, and, yes, Jesus is Lord. You asked about hidden pride. I will show you this. It is when you find yourself thinking Bob is not treating you right. It is when you find yourself insisting that he address you in a certain way and correcting him on how he has spoken to you. That is pride. You find it is more important to correct him than to try to understand what is going on with him. You need to just listen in those moments and try to be sympathetic to his needs.

You see, your way requires him to change, but God's way requires you to change. The latter requires you to put on a compassionate nature–one where you are listening not judging. Wait for him to finish, be agreeable, and allow Me to do the work on Bob. Your way causes him to be guarded and keeps him from communicating with you. It also has you doing the work. You don't allow room for Me to work. I am the One Who will give you comfort and security. Bob can't be perfect, but you expect him to be. It is hard on him. When you feel you have been mistreated, don't make a display, but come to Me. I will work on both of you. But I tell you the truth, if you continue to do what you have been doing, you will see no difference in your prideful behavior or in Bob's. Try this next time–just listen. When you feel anger, come to Me. I will work on your heart and on his. (See Hebrews 13:5, John 14:27)

I will further reveal why you react this way. Your reaction is from years of mistreatment when you didn't have a voice.

You couldn't express yourself because of all the powerful personalities in your family. Now, as an adult, you can and do express yourself but in a way that the other person has to be perfect. If they are not, you let them have it. It is ineffective to be this way because now you're the one with the powerful personality not allowing others to be themselves. You see how your forceful demands on others to treat you perfectly impose on them. Let people know they are free to make mistakes because you have the strength, grace, and mercy to love them no matter what. (See Proverbs 11:2, Philippians 2:3)

God Mail: Love and Correction

This is God, and Jesus is Lord. You learned yesterday that your thoughts could be mixed with Mine. That can be a problem, but you, along with Bob, are learning to prove whether it is of you or of Me. You need words of encouragement today because what I ask of you is not easy. To die to yourself will be the hardest thing you've ever done. It is not easy to change from being a self-centered, non-Christian to a self-sacrificing servant of the Lord. It is a large task, but you are praying for Me to help—expecting I will. You do believe that I will show you the way, and that is good. Many begin to feel helpless and give up hope. Keep seeking. You will find My grace, My mercy, and, most of all, My love. (See Matthew 7:7-8)

Now you are beginning to realize there is another side to My love. If I only showed you one side, My love, then you would not be moved to change as dramatically as is needed. There has to be a judgment side to go along with the love side. Balance—remember this. Now with love there is judgment, but this is not human judgment. God's justice is different than what you have experienced in the world. God's judgment is always just. Remember this; it is a truth of God. So, knowing that God's judgment is always just, when judgment comes, you will not think it is unfair. It can't be because it is My judgment, and you will remember it is always fair. In order to work Christ's character in you, as you truly desire, it requires both My love and My judgment.

In the past when judgment has come to you from the world, it has crushed you. So much so, that your defense was to retreat and to feel useless and unworthy of love. When I bring correction, remember it is all to work the character of Christ in you. I never withdraw My love. I love you no matter what (unconditionally). So you know My love is constant, and My judgment is always fair. Repeat this when correction comes. (See Hebrews 12:6-11)

You can't be perfect. Just love Me and keep seeking Me. Know that My judgment is only used to bring you closer to the likeness of Christ, but know that I will always love you. Run to Me, and I will wrap My arms around you. Now that you are clear on this, we will begin to work together. You will begin to experience more growth in the knowledge of Christ and in His character. You will begin to encounter more of My judgment, but you will not despair knowing that My love is there to strengthen you. Come closer with no fear. It is good that you are seeking a closer walk with Me. You will see that this is necessary for Christ to be more visible in you—for His nature to become greater so that your nature becomes less. (See Galatians 2:20)

Chapter Thirteen

To Know Each Other

What is the definition of fellowship? A synonym would be companionship. Companionship means to be in someone's company, habitually. We are actually called to be in fellowship with God through Jesus Christ according to First Corinthians 1:9. So if God is calling us into fellowship with Him and if this means we are to be His companions, don't you think He wants to talk to us?

When I first began spending time with God, I was doing all the talking. I was desperate to be free from my old life of moodiness and depression. And praise God, about a year from the date I claimed my healing from depression, I was free.

By trusting God's Word and exchanging my fears for His power, love, and sound mind, I marveled at God's ability to supernaturally heal my heart and mind. I began to search the Scriptures for more of His promises. My husband knew a lot of the Word, but I had not ventured into the Word very deeply. I read others' interpretation of the Bible, but for me to read and understand the Bible was hard. However, I decided to begin my first independent study of the Word in the book of John. Many had told me this book dealt with the love of God, and I knew I needed to know much more about God's love.

I got as far as John 10 (NIV) entitled "The Shepherd and His Flock" and could go no further. Verse 27 said very plainly, *"My sheep listen to my voice; I know them, and they follow me."* "Hey," I thought to myself quite literally, "Why can't I hear God's voice?" That question caused me to read everything I could about hearing God's voice. This led me to seeking the "gifts of the Spirit."

As I told you earlier, I spent four months pursuing, pleading, and, yes, begging God for these gifts. I did not really understand what these gifts were about, but I found myself desiring them, especially the gift of prophecy. I just knew if they were available, I wanted them. I was tireless in my study of others' opinions in this area and let my own study of the Word end. I prayed long and hard in the Spirit until that day I heard, "I say they are there, and they are there."

Once I realized what the Lord was telling me, I understood that God had already given me everything through Jesus. It was not about getting from God; He had already given me all. It was about a hardened heart that made it difficult for me by faith to believe and to receive His precious gifts. As I continued to study, I received more assurances that He definitely would speak to me.

Those assurances began with the accident in the convenience store's parking lot. I began to recognize more often the unction (prompting) of God's Spirit. This knowing in my spirit would direct me and show me things God wanted me to do.

One day I was sure I was to give someone $100. This was above my regular tithing. God had already wrestled with me concerning tithing, and He won. But He didn't say anything about giving above and beyond my tithe! Immediately, I began to reason away giving the $100. Why would I give this person $100?

Later that day, I went to the bank to withdrawal my usual biweekly allowance of $100. However, instead of writing $100 on the withdraw form, I wrote $200. I had no intention of doing that. Needless to say, I gave away the extra $100 as God had asked.

This happened more than once. In fact, the next time I wavered about giving, an additional zero was involved. I heard the Lord tell me to give a ministry $1000, but I was sure I didn't hear Him correctly. As I made out the check for $100, my hand wrote an additional zero. I knew that it was God, so I gave the $1000.

Chapter Fourteen

Listening Prayer

After receiving interpretation for my prayer language, "I say they are there, and they are there," I was on fire. I ordered more books on the gifts of the Spirit. In one of the orders I received, I was given a free gift. It was the book, *Hearing from God* (previously titled *Listening Prayer*), by Mary Ruth Swope. To my utter delight, the book was about hearing and discerning God's voice. I quickly got to work pouring over its pages.

The supernatural way in which this book was delivered into my hands gave me all the assurance I needed to believe that God wanted to speak to me in a clear voice. As I read this book, knowing that it was the key to my breakthrough, Mary Ruth Swope showed me how to listen for God's voice. I stopped doing all the talking in prayer and became quiet so that I could hear His voice. It did not happen immediately. In fact, it did not happen during my usual prayer time. The first time I heard my Father's voice was in my car on the way to work one morning. Until now I had just received passing thoughts (a knowing), but this was an actual conversation. The voice sounded like mine, but the words were filled with wisdom and authority.

That morning on the way to work, I had been praying in tongues for the salvation of my family members. I was crying and praising God for what He would do for them. Then I stopped, got quiet, and heard God speak. He told me to examine my motives for why I was praying for the salvation of my family. He explained that while it was right to pray for their salvation, I needed to consider whether I wanted them saved to make my life easier or to make their lives easier.

In just a few loving words, He showed me that I was praying for selfish reasons. I wanted my family to stop hurting me, and I knew the only one who could change that situation was God. However, He could see my heart and knew my motives were more about me than about them. Those words ministered to my hardness of heart, and true compassion for my family rose out of my spirit. I am happy to say that these compassionate prayers, along with my mother's and Blanky's prayers, have lead to the salvation of others in my family. God didn't override their free will because of our prayers, but He went to work in their lives much the same as He did in mine before my salvation.

I, of course, was flying high after the Lord delivered this message in such a clear and direct fashion. I had believed for months that I could hear from Him this way, but I never imagined what it would be like or how it would change me forever.

Chapter Fifteen

The Wrong Spirit

Did you ever hear that too much of the Bible makes you dry up; too much of the Spirit makes you blow up; but a balance between the two makes you grow up? I can tell you from firsthand experience, it is true. I had been floating along in the Spirit, and, to be perfectly honest, I was becoming a little goofy. Bob, on the other hand, had very little experience with the things of the Spirit of God, but he had a lot of knowledge of the Word of God. I believe one reason God put us together was to create balance in us.

As I said, I was ecstatic about hearing God's voice, but I became careless. Not more than a day later, I had a very odd experience. I believed I was again hearing from God, but this time I sensed something different–lack of peace. I became frightened of shadows, and I would jump when I heard noises in the house. I ignored these red flags because I believed I was hearing from God, and that was all I cared to believe. I accepted anything I heard as the Gospel, never confirming anything in the Word of God.

For a week I got up at 3 o'clock in the morning to receive these messages. I allowed this spirit to speak to me about the mighty works I would do. I was commanded not to tell Bob about this but was assured that he would be told later of the marvelous things that we would do for God. I became full of pride instead of love and compassion. And with pride comes the fall, and I fell hard.

After a week the spirit said it would tell Bob that day of things it told me. I was so excited that I hurried home from work and waited for Bob. When he arrived home, I expected him to be just as excited as I was upon hearing from God. He did not say a word about this all evening, but I waited patiently all the same.

That same day we received a tape in the mail from one of the ministries we support. On that tape the man explained that in the last days even the greatest men and women of God could be deceived. He explained further that without being properly grounded in the Word of God, it would be difficult to see the red flags of deception. I listened as this man of God warned of false prophets and how important it was to confirm all that you hear by the Word of God.

I began to cry because I recognized what I had opened myself up to that week. I continued to cry as I told Bob about the spirit and what it had told me. He very calmly and gently led me to Scriptures that contradicted what I had heard. We prayed together, bound this spirit of deception, and cast it to hell in Jesus name.

Then with a strength that could have come only from God, I made a profession of faith. I spoke out my belief that God would teach me how to hear and discern His voice so that I would be able to use His words to help others. I thanked God for showing me that even though I got caught up in pride and in my selfish desires, He was faithful to deliver me from evil. It was not a coincidence that the tape on deception arrived that day. I further thanked Him for the promise that He turns all things to good that Satan intends for destruction. (See Genesis 50:20 and Nehemiah 13:2) God has honored this prayer beyond my wildest dreams.

God Mail: Engrafted Word of God

This is your Lord Jesus. I have been with you for many years. I have never had you from My sight. You are Mine, and I am yours forever. Of this you can be sure. I love you and intend only good for you, so you can trust the words you are receiving today. I have been watching a child of God crawl, walk, and now run. You and yours are called to a place in Christ where much is required, but the desire that the Father God has placed in you is great.

You are to continue in the Word—growing in the knowledge of who you serve. You are to learn My Word that has been hidden deep within you. As you read, the Word is drawn out, and the Holy Spirit reveals the meaning. You see how it is? The Word has already been planted in you. I am there, but it is yours to dig for the meaning of the Word within you. It is yours to have light shed on it as you yield to the Spirit of God. Let His light shine on the Seed, the engrafted Word of God within you.

When you hear something for the first time, often you have a witness in your spirit—the born-again spirit. The Word in you, which may not have had light shown on it yet, reacts. Based on your knowledge of the Word and on the influences that you allow when interpreting the Word of God, the engrafted Word of God reacts. Through steady exposure to light, the engrafted Word of God begins to take root in your heart.

You see the completed work of Jesus has been planted in you. It is yours to let the Holy Spirit reveal it, and yours to meditate on the Word so that the engrafted Word takes root in your heart. (See James 1:21) Where is Jesus? Where does the Holy Spirit live? Where is God at work today in this earth? The answer to these questions is in your heart and the hearts of all who have let Jesus become their Savior. This is the way it is. I have given you all things for godliness. It was planted in your heart the day you asked Jesus into your heart. He is that Seed that was planted that day. He is the engrafted Word of God. (See I Peter 1:22-23)

You heard of a man (a nonbeliever) who was chosen to play a part in a movie as one of God's most powerful prophets, Moses. You heard him speak of the confusion that he and many others see in the Bible. To them it is a puzzle. You remember yourself that it was hard to read and to understand. The time is now for the children of God to take the engrafted Word of God and to make a demand on it. That demand is to reveal, through the Spirit of wisdom, revelation, and knowledge of the Bible, the truths of the Almighty God in Whom you serve. (See Ephesians 1:17-19)

It is time to show the entire Word of God, not just bits and pieces. For those who diligently ask, seek, and knock, they will see the deep treasures of truth in My Word. They will guide and teach others by My Spirit. (See Matthew 7:7-9) Teaching others how to mine My Word for themselves will unlock the great treasures locked in their hearts. Trust Me and lean not on your own understanding, and you will know through heart knowledge—the engrafted Word of God made alive—the knowledge that will set you, along with countless others, free. (See John 8:31-32)

Chapter Sixteen

Discerning God's Voice

After the victory over the deceiving spirit, I believed more strongly than ever that God would speak to me as clearly and as casually as you would with a friend at your kitchen table. I went back to Mary Ruth Swope's book, *Hearing from God*, but this time I looked for information concerning discernment. I was hearing voices, but I needed to know how to discriminate between God's voice and the other voices.

Also, I reread John 10 several more times. I focused on John 10:2-5 (NIV) that states,

> *The man who enters by the gate is the shepherd of his sheep. The watchman opens the gate for him, and the sheep listen to his voice. He calls his own sheep by name and leads them out. When he has brought them out all his own, he goes on ahead of them, and his sheep follow him because they know his voice. But they will never follow a stranger; in fact, they will run away from him because they do not recognize a stranger's voice.*

According to this Scripture, it promises us the ability to discern the difference between the voice of God and some other voice from the spirit realm. My faith and belief for this God-given ability was sure.

With the Scriptures Mary Ruth Swope cited in her book, I began to search the Bible for more evidence of God's will in this area. Then one day my Bible literally fell open to the Scripture that would forever change my ability to discern God's voice. First John 4:1-2 and 13-15 (NIV) says,

> *Dear friends, do not believe every spirit, but test the spirits to see whether they are from God, because many false prophets have gone out into the world. This is how you can recognize the Spirit of God: Every spirit that acknowledges that Jesus Christ has come in the flesh is from God... We know that we live in him and he in us, because he has given us of his Spirit. And we have seen and testify that the Father has sent his Son to be the Savior of the world. If anyone acknowledges that Jesus is the Son of God, God lives in him and he in God.*

Later, I found another Scripture that was helpful in discerning God's voice. In First Corinthians 12:3 (KJ) I read,

> *Wherefore I give you to understand, that no man speaking by the Spirit of God calleth Jesus ac-*

cursed: and [that] no man can say that Jesus is the Lord, but by the Holy Ghost.

In April 1999, I continued practicing *listening prayer*. The difference this time was that I insisted I hear Jesus lifted up as Lord and Savior. God was faithful to answer this request. By the end of April, God encouraged me to start writing down the messages I was receiving, and He instructed Bob and I to confirm them through His Word.

We also followed the advice given in *Hearing from God* by Mary Ruth Swope (pp. 74-75) and made sure the messages had these five qualities. The message should cause you to turn to God, respect and adore Him, and turn away from evil (See Job 28:28); increase your faith, knowledge, and understanding of the Scriptures (See Proverbs 4:7); result in actions that yield spiritual fruit (See James 3:17); strengthen you (See Colossians 1:11); and give you such joy that you want to praise and thank God (See Colossians 1:12).

Since 1999, I have received over 400 messages. They are filled with His knowledge, understanding and wisdom. And because the messages are filled with His thoughts, they have been a blessing, not only to me but also to countless others.

While His Spirit inspires the messages, please do not get the idea that they are perfect. It says in First Corinthians 14:32 (NIV) that, *"The spirits of the prophets are subject to the control of prophets."* I know this is true because I can see parts of my personality in the messages. Also, I know that the wording and grammar in the messages are not perfect. That is not due to God's lack of knowledge and skill in those areas but rather to my lack of knowledge and skill.

The first messages were about the love of God. God was doing a major renovation on my heart. In one of the most important messages to me personally, He told me I was no longer "this property condemned" but "this property under construction." This message reassured me that I was His child forever. It helped me to understand that God loved me for "who I am" and not for "what I do." (NOTE: The message, *This Property Under Construction*, has been included at the end of this chapter. I have written personal notes to demonstrate how Bob and I test the messages through Scripture. Also, I explain how the message meets the five qualities Mary Ruth Swope recommends.)

Over the years, the subject matter of the messages has varied depending on my needs and on the needs of others. One of most exciting aspects of my *listening prayer* experience is how it has established my faith in God's Word. He has caused John 10 to come alive. I am now living the Scripture, "My sheep will know My voice." I am more able to recognize His voice, and, with each new day, our fellowship time brings more revelation of Him. I can honestly say I am coming to know Him as my friend and my companion. I not only know His voice, but He knows mine and hears it amid the throng of people that enter His throne room each day.

God Mail: *This Property under Construction*

This is your Lord Jesus, the lifter of your head, and the One in Whom *all hope* is given. It is your hope in salvation that cries out of your spirit man. It is the hope that you are crying for when you hear of lost salvation. You know that hopelessness leads to depression. What better tool of the devil than to let the body of Christ believe in lost salvation? It has a dual effect.

On one hand, those who believe in lost salvation think they would never lose it *because of pride in their own self-righteousness*. That is why with boldness they speak on such matters as losing salvation. On the other hand, there are those who would *lose the hope of salvation* upon hearing that salvation has to be kept. You are the one who has believed wholeheartedly upon the hope, and it is to that hope you cry. Without the hope of your salvation, you are lost. It is the "loss of hope" that should be taught. You see, if Satan can have you believe that salvation can be lost, he can then have you lose hope and let depression settle in your spirit. (Depression is a spirit, but when I speak of letting it settle in your spirit, I'm speaking of its effects on your spirit. I am not saying that it possesses your spirit.) So it is about hope that you grieve.

When you hear about lost salvation, your emotions react, and it passes through your spirit. Your human spirit does not receive it; therefore, you reject its effects. But your emotional reaction is based on your desire to have truth told in the body of Christ. You see the ill effects of the message concerning lost salvation to those who would receive it.

There is a cleansing and renewal upon salvation that is real and genuine. It is like seeing a newborn baby cooing and babbling and smiling. A fresh breeze is blown in them and upon them. You recognize this as the Holy Spirit taking up residence in them. Then the Holy Spirit starts a remodeling project. And you know that before the home begins to look finished, there is first a big messy period of time before the finish. That is how it is when the temple of the Lord is under construction—a mess before the finish. (See I John 3 and John 10:27-30)

Many in the body of Christ are constantly under construction and grow weary. However, notice that the property is no longer "this property condemned" but "this property under construction." There is a big difference. A property condemned means hopelessness—doomed to be torn down and carried off to a consuming fire. All of it is burned away. However, with a property under construction, there is the hope of its completion. Yes, there are times when the house looks worse than when the reconstruction started, but, in the end, there is always the expected outcome of completion. The hope is constant even in the midst of the mess.

You see the analogy very clearly. It is *in the hope* that faith rises up within the spirit of man. Your spirit has taken hold of the promise and the hope. That is what grieves you when you hear messages on lost salvation. It grieves your spirit when people, who suggest that salvation is something that comes and goes, cheapen the cost that was paid so that you could receive salvation. It is the hope of salvation that many do not understand. That is why it is necessary to separate who a person becomes upon salvation from what that person does. Remember there is a vast difference from being "this property condemned" and "this property under construction." (See Romans 7:15-25 and 8:1-2)

Special Commentary about the Message: This Property under Construction

The following are personal notes I made to demonstrate how I confirm messages from God using both Scripture and the five qualities recommended by Mary Ruth Swope.

In the first paragraph of the message, notice the mention of Jesus as Lord according to First Corinthians. God has always been faithful to say this so that I know it is the Holy Spirit and not another spirit.

This message helped me to understand how Scripture concerning salvation can appear to contradict itself. When I received salvation, it never occurred to me that salvation could be lost. The first time I heard this idea was in a church service, and it nearly killed me. I was struck with terror thinking that somehow salvation could be stripped away, and I would be plunged back into darkness. I was told I would have to work to keep it, and here I had thought I was safe: eternally saved, justified, and cleansed of all my sins by the blood of Jesus Christ.

In First John 2:27-29 and 3:1-5, you can see that through Jesus our spirits are born again. Thus, God becomes our Father, and we become His children. Our spirit man is complete and perfect in God's sight. With hope in Jesus Christ, we are justified (in right standing with God—just as if we never sinned). We no longer have a sin nature. Yes, our souls (minds, wills, and emotions) are still being perfected, but, in our spirits, we are the very likeness of Jesus Christ.

If you continue reading in First John 3, you might get the idea that by continuing to sin after salvation (the Amplified Bible uses the word, *"habitually"*), salvation can be lost. But that idea would contradict John 10:27-30 that assures Christians that they have been given eternal life *forever*. They are in His hands, and no one can take them from Him (not even a believer's own foolish behavior).

Christians who are in pride think that they can keep their own salvation by works, and they wholeheartedly think they have stopped repeatedly sinning. But what they fail to realize is that anything not of faith is sin (Romans 14:23). Let me ask you this. Have you completely stopped worrying about your finances, your children, or your health? Since your salvation, have you stopped gossiping, overeating, or becoming angry?

As for Christians whose *hope* in salvation is dashed by hearing they have to work to keep salvation, they become hopeless and give up because they cannot stop sinning. You see, both situations are focused on a sin-consciousness not a God-consciousness.

In my own life I continue to struggle with personal sin in certain areas, but I know God is still pleased with me. First John 3 is not talking about personal sin but about the sin nature (habitually sinning). As children of God, we have been born into God's nature (righteousness through grace). So, no, I do not habitually sin because I no longer have a sin nature (a sin-consciousness). I have God's nature (a God-consciousness) because of who I am in Jesus Christ. Yes, I still deal with personal sin but in the light of who I am in Jesus—100% accepted and loved by the Father.

God showed me through this message that I have gone from "this property condemned" (a sinner with Satan's nature) to "this property under construction" (a sinless, guiltless child of God with His nature). With this message, I saw three spiritual conditions:

1. *Condemned* (children of the devil, spiritually dead)
2. *Under construction* (children of God embracing the hope of salvation; having a God-consciousness; focusing on who they are not what they do; doing the work of God out of "a want to" because of a love for God and not out of "a have to" because they are trying to continually earn righteousness and keep salvation)
3. *Construction halted* (children of God that are either self-righteous or have lost their hope of salvation; both hanging onto a sin-consciousness).

This may help to explain Paul's seemingly confusing ramblings about his old and new nature in Romans 7:15-24.

But continue reading in Romans 7:25 and 8:1-2. In Christ we are righteous. We must remember our righteousness in Him, or we will begin to let the sin-consciousness condemn us— halting the construction God is doing in us. Yes, we as Christians look messy at times, but it is the hope of completion (the perfecting of our souls) that is our joy and peace.

Earlier in the chapter I mentioned Mary Ruth Swope's five qualities that each message should possess. Do you recognize them in the message?

1. I am more in love with God and respect Him even more because of how He has assured me of my eternal salvation through Jesus Christ. I want to serve Him out of love, not fear of rejection.
2. The revelation through this message helps me to better understand seemingly conflicting Scripture.
3. Love, peace, and joy fill my heart knowing that I am eternally His.
4. It gives me strength knowing that if I mess up, He still loves me.
5. I rejoice knowing that I can run to Him no matter what happens or how I behave.

Chapter Seventeen

The Desires of Thine Heart

God has a promise for every believer. According to Jeremiah 29:11, He tells us that He has a plan for our lives, and it is a good plan. But how can you know His plan unless you spend time with Him? I cannot tell you how important it is to spend time with God. He wants to impart to us His knowledge, understanding, wisdom, and ability so that He can send us out to minister to others through His Word. But if you do not know Him and cannot hear Him, how can He get His plan to you?

I can remember my husband saying that for years he was concerned that God would send him to a far off land. Bob did not really seek God for God's plan. Bob wanted to do for God what Bob wanted to do and then hoped that God would bless it. But what we are now finding out is that God will not give you something to do for Him without first planting that desire in your heart.

For a long time, I did not understand Scriptures such as Matthew 6:33 and Psalm 37:4 (KJ).

> *But seek ye first the kingdom of God, and His righteousness; and all these things shall be added unto you.... Delight thyself also in the Lord; and He shall give thee the desires of thine heart.*

I saw those desires only as the ones I had. I looked at God as a big slot machine. I thought all I had to do was to put in my prayers and out would pop what I wanted.

Now, as I have grown in knowledge, understanding, and wisdom that only come from fellowship with the Father, I understand what these Scriptures mean. If I seek the kingdom of God (His way of doing things) and if I remember that it is only through the righteousness of Jesus that I can fellowship with Him, I can then receive His desires for me. What is even more remarkable is that the desires I once had for material prosperity have lessened. I now want the spiritual wealth that only God can provide. He has placed desires in my heart that far surpass anything I could have thought or even hoped for.

This book is one of those desires He planted in my heart. When it was first prophesied that I would write a book, I actually laughed out loud. I had written a lot in college, so I knew how difficult writing was for me. So to me, a book meant many hours of labor and pain.

However, here I am writing this book. It has not been difficult, but has been truly a labor of love. I see now how fellowship with the Father has brought my desires in line with His plan for me. No, this does not mean I have become a robot and no longer have a choice. But as I spend time with Him, the things that I thought were impossible have become possible. The things that I thought I would hate have become passions.

When you spend time with Him, you cannot help but be transformed into the likeness of His Son. Jesus becomes more a part of you. Galatians 2:20 (Amp) tells us:

> *I have been crucified with Christ [in Him I have shared His crucifixion]; it is no longer I who live, but Christ (the Messiah) lives in me; and the life I now live in the body I live by faith in (by adherence to and reliance on and complete trust in) the Son of God, Who loved me and gave Himself up for me.*

When you die to your own selfish desires and begin to let God have His way in you, life becomes so easy. Yes, you still have the struggles and disappointments that living in this world bring. But when you are close to God and know Him intimately, you have an assurance that He will make a way out of every situation. The best part is the joy in watching Him at work in your life. Everyday with Him is an adventure.

If you are truly sensitive to His ways, you can recognize Him in the smallest details of your life. Try it! Ask for a convenient parking space. Hey, I prayed for socks, and look how He has blessed me. He will do the same for you!

Chapter Eighteen

Practicing Listening Prayer

At this point, I believe it would be helpful to share with you how I prepare to listen for God's voice. I purposely and faithfully set aside time for God. I get up early in the morning and go to my prayer room that I have equipped with Bibles, Christian reading materials and music, a computer, and a comfortable couch. The amount of time I spend with God before listening for His voice varies, as do the activities. By having no set pattern, my prayer time never becomes rote and monotonous. I may start with praise and worship, or reading either the Word or other books, or praying in either my known language or my prayer language. However I begin, I will eventually be in His glorious presence. While in His presence, I become quiet and listen for His voice.

To help me hear clearly from God, I have adopted the suggestions made in Mary Ruth Swope's book, *Hearing from God* (p. 207). They are:

1. **"Getting right with God."** To me this means that I ask God to show me things that would cause me to not hear His

voice clearly. I may be convicted of unforgiveness or of something I said or did that has hardened my heart. I have learned that beating myself up over these things is not what God wants. He wants me to recognize these things and repent (turn from them). So I remind myself that only through the righteousness of Jesus can I come to God. I know that I am His child whom He loves. I ask Him to help me turn from anything that causes me to be out of fellowship with Him and then rely on His strength to change my heart.

2. **"Getting tough with the Devil."** I bind the demon spirits that are maneuvering against me and cast them out in Jesus' Mighty name. I also bind my thoughts and ask to hear only the thoughts of God by His Spirit.

3. **"Getting quiet within."** In the quiet of my room and of my mind, I listen for Him. The voice sounds like mine, but the thoughts and words are beyond my natural understanding. The main thing is that I *expect* Him to speak, and He does.

During this time, He will reveal to me His thoughts concerning His Word, a situation, etc. For example, I may have read something in His Word that I don't understand, so God will explain it in a way He knows I will understand. Often He will use examples from nature or from my own personal experiences.

Many times He will give me messages concerning others. No matter how insignificant those messages seem to me, the people they are intended for get blessed. Usually they respond with tears of gratitude and joy because the messages assure them that God is working to answer their prayers.

As you practice *listening prayer*, you will begin to hear His voice throughout your day. The word "practice" is not a word I hear often in the Christian community. However, I have found that only through practicing have I become better able to yield to His Spirit, to quiet my mind, and to listen for His voice during the day.

I often pondered how it would be possible to fulfill the Scripture, *"pray without ceasing"* (I Thessalonians 5:17 [KJ]). Now I understand through experience that as one's mind becomes set on the things of God (having the mind of Christ), one begins to hear His voice constantly. The problem for us lies in *"casting down imaginations, and every high thing that exalteth itself against the knowledge of God, and bringing into captivity every thought to the obedience of Christ"* (II Corinthians 10:5 [KJ]). I believe *listening prayer* is one of the vital keys to praying without ceasing.

Chapter Nineteen

You Can Hear

As I tell people about my experience, I have come to realize that many Christians have not heard about *listening prayer*. They seem to think that hearing God's voice is only for a chosen few. But John 10 makes known to believers that God wants to speak to them personally.

Why is it that so many do not? Mary Ruth Swope (p. 52) suggests seven reasons why:

1. *Lack of faith to believe that hearing from God is for today.*
2. *Lack of a strong commitment to Jesus Christ as Lord of their life.*
3. *The presence of unconfessed sin and a "double standard" lifestyle.*
4. *Ignorance of the scriptural evidence of the believer's privilege to hear from God personally.*
5. *Lack of teaching on how to pursue such a listening prayer experience.*

6. *Fear of being called a "religious fanatic" or "mentally ill."*
7. *Fear of being open to the "wrong spirits" or being led astray by the enemy.*

As you read this list, you may have identified with one or more reasons that are keeping you from one of the most rewarding experiences one can have with God. I know that lack of knowledge was one reason my husband could not hear from God personally. Another reason was worry. He had difficulty casting his cares upon the Lord and freeing his mind from worry so that he could hear God's sure, clear voice. So you can imagine his reluctance to pursue *listening prayer* when he saw me deceived by a wrong spirit.

However, one day when we were praying together, I heard God say He would speak. I began to write the message. Bob watched me write as quickly as my hand could move. I wrote four pages in moments, and when I read it back, the wording was almost perfect. He saw that I didn't go into a trance or act spooky and weird. I just heard God say He would speak, believed that He would, and took action–I wrote.

In James 1:22 we are commanded to put action to God's Word. I believe that writing down these messages is the necessary action He requires of me. Also, by writing the messages, Bob and I are better able to confirm them through His Word.

As Bob's belief in hearing God's voice became stronger, he began to practice *listening prayer*. However, it was very difficult for him because of random thoughts that would not allow him to be still in his mind. He did not experience victory in *listening prayer* until God revealed to him his tendency to worry. Also, Bob had to learn how to bind the specific demon spirit of confusion.

During this time we attended a conference in Tulsa. One of the workshops was "The Gift of the Spirit: Prophecy." The instructor taught God's Word in the area of the prophetic, and, by the end of the workshop, most people spoke out prophetic words. However, it was not until later that afternoon that Bob spoke prophetically. That experience further deepened his belief that God would speak to him personally.

Bob has continued practicing *listening prayer*. He sometimes becomes discouraged that he doesn't hear as easily as I do. However, he has remarked that his mind is now free from worry and is at peace. He has allowed God to take his cares, especially those for his children. I have seen him grow closer to God through *listening prayer*s. As a result, he is more lighthearted; therefore, more of his prayer time is spent praising and worshipping God instead of worrying.

I know that since I have begun to hear from God, my ability to believe, receive, and do for Him has grown tremendously. It amazes me that I could have ever thought He was cruel and cold. Now I know Him, and He is abounding in love and compassion. There are times when I come to Him and envision myself crawling up on His lap. I can imagine His arms around me. What I hear is this: "I love you, little one. Come here. Let us walk together in the cool of the evening." I am reduced to tears every time.

God Mail: The Light of the World

This is God, and Jesus, your Lord, is here. He sees your heart, and yes, it is the heart that is perfect. It is the soul and the body that are lacking and keeping people from the blessings of God. Believe, however, that it is the heart of the believer that your God looks upon to see their desires. The flesh is whimsical, but the heart's desire is steady and true. Shield not the heart on your own, but let your God bring light into every crevice.

To shed the light of God into the heart of the believer is to bring the knowledge of God and His ways to the believer. Understand that only through the knowledge and the goodness of God can one experience what God has in store for him. It is the willingness to make yourself totally available that brings great victory into your life. Yielding to the Spirit of God is the only way that your life can be the light.

"This little light of mine, I'm going let it shine," is a song for the very young but a powerful song. It is a song of hope and of willingness to be the hope for others. It is a song to share the good news that God in heaven is the way to a rich, full life. It is a song to make known that the Son of the God in heaven is the only way to the Father; therefore, Jesus is that light. The light illuminates the pathway to the Father. Though it is a narrow pathway, there is room for all. The pathway is not yet full.

My Son left so that the Holy Spirit could come and transform believers into the light. Now it is those with the indwelling of My Spirit who light the path. So being the light of the world falls on all who believe. My Spirit, the Son of the Most High in you, lights the way for all. So this little light of mine is Jesus living in you–guiding the way to the Father. Be that little light that illuminates the world–showing the world the sin nature. But also showing there is a better way–a way that brings blessings and happiness. Blessings and happiness only experienced through knowing the Son of the Most High and accepting what He has done.

"This little light of mine…" Although many have tried to claim this light as their own, you know that it is the light of Jesus in you that shines so bright. It is God's love in you that shines so bright. It is the Holy Spirit's ministry in you that illuminates the way. "This little light of God the Father, the Son, and the Holy Spirit, I'm going to let it shine." Yes, the second half of this is your part. You are the one who determines if it shines or not. You are also the one who determines if it is a flickering flame or a bonfire. *Be a bonfire!* (See Matthew 5:1-16)